School:
Then and Now

by Marianne Lenihan

PEARSON

Scott
Foresman

Editorial Offices: Glenview, Illinois • Parsippany, New Jersey • New York, New York
Sales Offices: Needham, Massachusetts • Duluth, Georgia • Glenview, Illinois
Coppell, Texas • Ontario, California • Mesa, Arizona

ISBN: 0-328-13165-2

7 8 9 10 V010 14 13 12 11 10 09 08

"Older children, please take out your hornbooks. Younger children, please recite your numbers."

If you were a student in the early days of the United States, that is how your school day might have started.

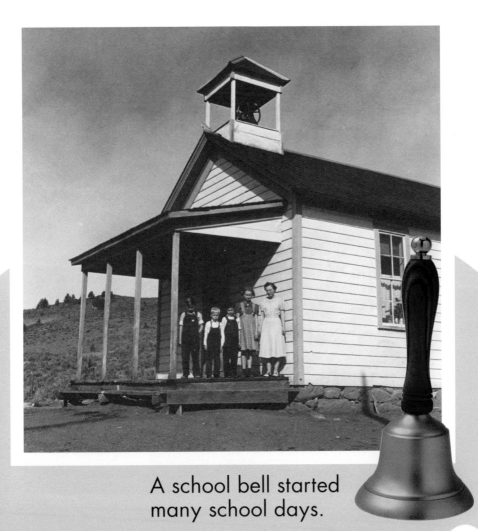

A school bell started many school days.

School was very different then. Not every child went to school. The children who went to school were all in the same room, no matter how old they were. They even shared the same teacher! The children sat in groups on wooden benches. They practiced reading and writing. They did math too.

Today in the United States, all children must go to school. Children are in classrooms with other children who are about the same age.

Now children learn how to read and write and do math just like children in earlier times. Children today study many other subjects too. All school children are taught to respect others.

Imagine schools with no books! Most students of long ago had only hornbooks. Hornbooks were not really books at all!

A hornbook looked like a wooden paddle. The alphabet and numbers were carved into one side. A sheet of paper was attached to the other side.

Hornbooks

Most students today go to schools that are filled with things to help them learn and play. There are books and computers and maps. There are writing pads and pencils and crayons. There are playgrounds and gyms.

Sometimes students of the past had to go far to get to school. Many walked a long way. Today most students ride school buses or are driven in cars.

After school many children long ago had chores to do to help their families. Children today often have time to play when the school day is over.

A schoolhouse

Schools are very different today than they were a long time ago. But something very important happened in schools long ago, and it still happens in schools today—learning!

Now Try This

Practice Like a Student of Long Ago

Copy these activities onto a piece of paper. Suppose you are a student of long ago.

Fill in the missing letters and numbers.

Activity

A B ___ D E F G ___ ___ J
K ___ M N O ___ ___ ___ S
___ ___ V ___ ___ Y ___

1 2 3 ___ ___ 6 7 ___ ___ ___ 11 ___
___ 14 ___ ___ ___ ___ 19 ___